This book is for all the little boys and girls that feel unseen in this world. I see you and you are beautiful!

To my two monsters:
Jaylen, you are forever my one and only "unofficial book club buddy".
Ty, you will ALWAYS be my bacon!

Nothing in this world makes me happier than watching you two smile and laugh with each other.
I Love you MORE!!!

Written by Shannon C. Singleton
Illustrated by Ujala Shahid
Edited and book designed by Bryony van der Merwe

Published in 2024
by I Rise Publishing

I RISE
PUBLISHING

ISBN: 979-8-9900501-0-5

Jaylen & Ty's Adventures

Based on True Stories

QUIT
Following me!

Shannon C. Singleton

Illustrated by Ujala Shahid

I Rise Publishing

One late afternoon, Jaylen was playing quietly in his room when suddenly, he shouted,

"Quit following me!"

Mom rushed into his room in a panic and asked,
"Who's following you, Jaylen?"

"He was here,
but he's gone now,"
exclaimed Jaylen angrily.

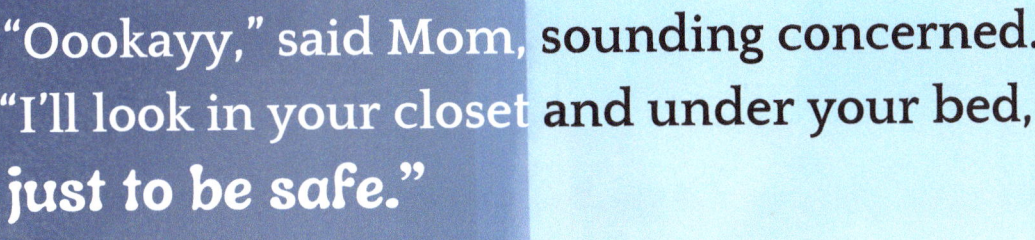

"Oookayy," said Mom, sounding concerned. "I'll look in your closet and under your bed, **just to be safe.**"

She did, but no one was there.

A few nights later,
as Jaylen walked down the hallway, he yelled,

"Stop following me!"

Dad raced to him from the living room and asked,

"Who's following you?"

"He was, but now he's gone."

Dad asked, **"What did he look like?"**

Jaylen couldn't quite answer the question. "He didn't look like you or me. He never talks. He just always

follows me around."

"This sounds a bit scary!"
Dad said, "Next time he comes, let me and Mom know as soon as you see him."

Jaylen nodded.

One night, Jaylen was playing in his room when his parents heard him shout,

"He's here!"

As his parents rushed in, Jaylen pointed and said,
"Look, he's right there!"

Their eyes followed
to where Jaylen pointed and saw that it was...

Jaylen's

Shadow!

They both sighed in relief.

"Jaylen, that is your shadow," Mom explained. "It's like when you see your reflection in the mirror, but it's made by the light shining on you. **Do you understand?**"

Jaylen shook his head from side to side. Mom thought for a few seconds and then smiled. "It will be better if **we show you.**"

Everyone followed Mom to the living room. Then she took one of the lamps off the table and plugged it into the wall close to Jaylen.

She turned the lamp on and then stood in front of it. Her Shadow stretched across the room. As she moved her left arm up and down, **her shadow did the same.**

Mom explained, "When the light comes from a certain angle, it makes a copy of you called a shadow. Whatever you do, **it does too."**

Jaylen's eyes widened as he started to
understand.

Dad added, "You can also use your hands and body to make different **shapes** and *images.*"

Jaylen was confused again.
"What do you mean?"

Dad placed his hands together in a
funny way in front of the light.
"The shadow looks like **a bird!**"
exclaimed Jaylen.

Jaylen giggled.

He and his parents made other shapes
and even added sounds to go with them!

Jaylen realized having his shadow follow
him wasn't bad at all.

The next time he saw his shadow,

he had loads of fun!

The Real Jaylen

Jaylen at 3 ½ years old

Keep the Adventure Going!

Bring Quit Following Me! to life with FREE guided lesson plans, printable activities, and complete Kindergarten, 1st Grade, and 2nd Grade curriculum.

Designed for families and classrooms, these ready-to-use resources help young readers think deeper, engage creatively, and extend the learning beyond the final page.

Scan the QR code below to get instant access!

subscribepage.io/eVpJeN

Other Works by This Author

Jaylen & Ty's Adventures series

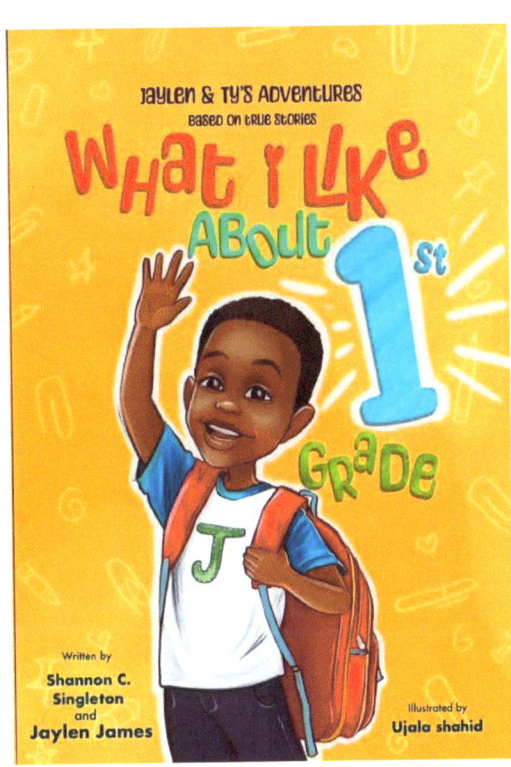

To learn more about each book, use the link or QR Code below.

https://www.irisepublishing.com/books/jaylen-tys-adventures-series

About the Author

Shannon Singleton has been mesmerized by books ever since she was able to read. Her fascination with them led to her love of writing when she took Mrs. Tureau's creative writing class in 7th grade.

She is the mother of two sons, Jaylen and Ty. From a young age, Jaylen also shared her passion for reading. His ability to devour books within a day or two was amazing! Through his reading, Jaylen quickly found there weren't many books available with African American protagonists as the main character or any black characters at all. Jaylen did not see himself in the books he read.

This is something Shannon also experienced. Due to this and other events, Shannon decided to be the change she wanted to see and wrote her own book series!

She hopes that the Jaylen and Ty's Adventures Based on True Stories series allows black boys and girls to see themselves represented in a positive way really early in their lives and also for the world to see them for who they truly are!

To learn more about Shannon use the link or QR code below.
https://www.irisepublishing.com/meet-our-authors/shannon-c-singleton

Facebook

Instagram

@SHANNONCSINGLETON_AUTHOR

A Word From the Author

I appreciate you taking the time to read my book with your little one (or by yourself – no judgment here! 🙃). If you enjoyed this book, it would mean a lot to me if you took a few minutes to leave a genuine review on the platform you purchased it from. Your thoughtful feedback is very important. Thank you for your time and support!

Shannon C. Singleton

www.ingramcontent.com/pod-product-compliance
Lightning Source LLC
Chambersburg PA
CBHW041452120626
46547CB00002B/423